# The Amazing Book of DINOSAURS

**Picture Credits:**

**Key: b-bottom, t-top, c-center, l-left, r-right**

**Stefano Azzalin:** cover tc, cover tcr, cover tr, 7r, 12cr, 17tl, 20cr, 22–23, 25t, 33t, 34b, 36–37, 44bl, 46br, 46–47; **Martin Bustamante**: cover tl, 8c, 10l, 20–21, 30l, 32–33, 40c, 42l, 42–43; **Juan Calle:** cover tcl, 12–13, 27cr, 30–31; **Mat Edwards:** profile box icons, 1, 4–5, 6–7, 8–9, 10–11, 14–15, 18–19, 24–25, 34–35, 38–39, 40–41; **Rudolf Farkas:** cover, 26–27; **Colin Howard:** 13cl; **Kunal Kundu**: 27tl, 44–45; **Jerry Pyke:** 4cr ; **Shutterstock:** 7b MikhailSh, 16cr Ozja, 18b Catmando, 21t watthanachai, 36b, 47cr Warpaint; **Parwinder Singh:** 38b; **Val Walerczuk:** 16–17; **Wikimedia Commons:** 5t mrwynd/ Denver Museum of Science and Nature, 9tr Didier Descouens/Peabody Museum of Natural History, 11t Didier Descouens, 22c Carol Abraczinskas, Paul C Sereno/ZooKeys, 22br Daderot/University of California Museum of Paleontology, 25cr Aimé Rutot, 31t American Museum of Natural History, 32l Allie Caulfield/Los Angeles Museum of Natural History, 34tr Dmitry Bogdanov/FunkMonk, 36tr Daderot/Natural History Museum of Utah, 40br Ra'ike/Museum am Löwentor, Stuttgart, 44tr James Erxleben/ British Museum.

ARCTURUS

This edition published in 2020 by Arcturus Publishing Limited
26/27 Bickels Yard, 151–153 Bermondsey Street,
London SE1 3HA



Author: Clare Hibbert
Editors: Joe Harris, Clare Hibbert, and Samantha Hilton
Designers: Amy McSimpson and Trudi Webb
Cover Design: Stefan Holliland

ISBN: 978-1-78950-835-2
CH007559NT
Supplier 29, Date 0620, Print run 10416

Printed in China

# The Amazing Book of DINOSAURS

## CONTENTS

# The Dinosaur Age

Dinosaurs appeared around 225 million years ago (mya) and ruled the land for over 160 million years. One of the best-known of the carnivorous, or meat-eating, dinosaurs was *Allosaurus*. Paleontologists have found more fossils of *Allosaurus* to study than of any other dinosaur. The first fossils were found in the late 19th century. The bones had honeycombed holes to make them lighter, just like birds' bones today.

## On Location

There are five known species of *Allosaurus*. Four were discovered in the Morrison Formation, a band of Late Jurassic rock in the western United States. The other comes from western Portugal's Lourinhã Formation.

## Famous Fossils

Swiss fossil hunter Kirby Siber and his team of dinosaur experts were responsible for finding two of the most complete *Allosaurus* specimens. Discovered in Wyoming in 1991, the skeleton of "Big Al" is 95 percent complete. The specimen was not fully grown and probably died of a bone infection. Five years later the team found an even more complete *Allosaurus*, which they named "Big Al Two." Its skull showed signs of injuries that had healed.

The long tail stuck out behind for balance.

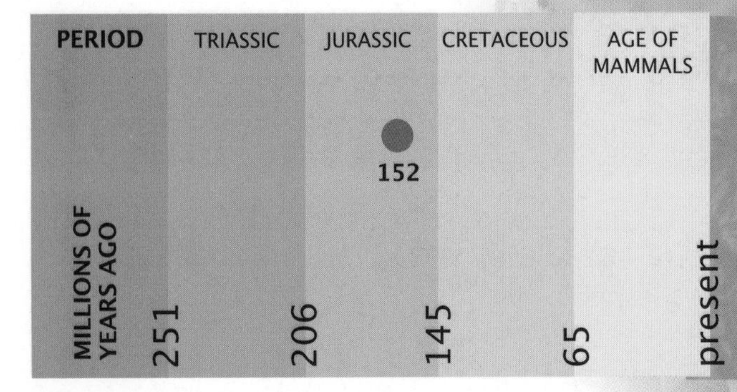


**Name:** *Allosaurus*
(AL-uh-SAWR-us)
**Family:** Allosauridae
**Height:** 5 m (16.5 ft)
**Length:** 12 m (40 ft)
**Weight:** 2.7 tonnes (3 tons)

**DINOSAUR PROFILE**

This *Allosaurus* skeleton is posed to take on *Stegosaurus* (pages 92–93).

Thick, sturdy legs supported its heavy bulk.

**_Allosaurus_ had long claws for gripping flesh.**

*Allosaurus* fed on carrion or its own kills.

# Archaeopteryx

Bird-like *Archaeopteryx* lived in what is now southern Germany around 150 million years ago. For many years it was the oldest-known bird, but in recent decades earlier feathered dinosaurs have been discovered. *Archaeopteryx* had flight feathers for gliding.

Some experts think *Archaeopteryx*'s wrists were not flexible enough for powered flight.

## Germany in the Late Jurassic

The landscape where *Archaeopteryx* lived was made up of low-lying islands among bodies of water, called lagoons. These lagoons had become separated from the nearby Tethys Ocean. When they dried up, the mud turned into limestone. Creatures that had sunk to the bottom were preserved as fossils.

*Archaeopteryx* was about the same size as a raven. It hunted frogs, lizards, dragonflies, and beetles.

**Flapping its wings while it was running helped *Archaeopteryx* to move faster.**

*Archaeopteryx*'s teeth were sharp and cone-shaped.

**Name:** *Archaeopteryx*
(Ar-kee-OP-ter-ix)
**Family:** Archaeopterygidae
**Length:** 30 cm (12 in)
**Wingspan:** 50 cm (20 in)
**Weight:** 1 kg (2.2 lb)

**Mesozoic dragonflies were huge, with wingspans up to 75 cm (30 in).**

*Archaeopteryx* means "ancient wing."

## Early Bird

The first feathered dinosaur ever discovered, *Archaeopteryx* was nicknamed the "first bird." It was clearly an early ancestor of birds because of its wing and tail feathers. However, it also had reptilian features—a long, bony tail, large hand claws, and jaws lined with sharp teeth.

An *Archaeopteryx* skeleton preserved in limestone

# Deinonychus

The dromaeosaur *Deinonychus* lived in North America during the Early Cretaceous. It probably hunted in packs to bring down prey much larger than itself. Its name means "terrible claw" and its killer weapon was the sickle-shaped claw on its second toe.

## Dangerous Family

Dromaeosaurs were formidable hunters. *Deinonychus* was medium-sized, about as large as a wolf. Its cousin *Utahraptor*, also from North America, was one of the largest species. It stood as tall as a person and was around 6 m (20 ft) long.

Working together, a team of *Deinonychus* could kill a juvenile *Tenontosaurus*. An adult was probably too large for them to attack.

### In a Flap

Like all dromaeosaurs, *Deinonychus* had feathers. Experts believe that feathers evolved from reptilian scales that had frayed and grown fluffy. They helped dinosaurs to stay warm. In time, feathers were used for display, too. It is possible that *Deinonychus* juveniles could even fly from danger by flapping their arms.

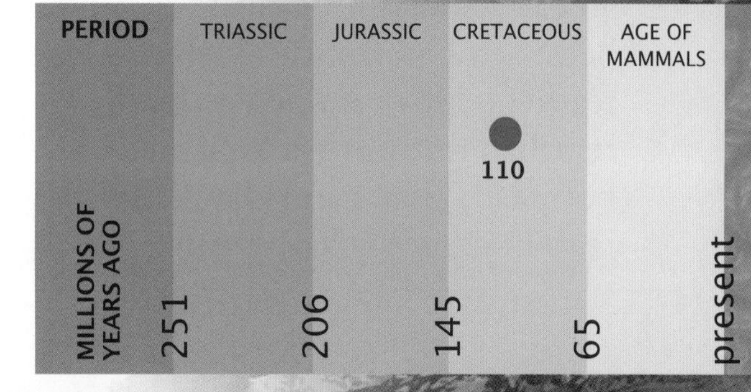


**Name:** *Deinonychus* (Dye-NON-ik-us)
**Family:** Dromaeosauridae
**Height:** 1.2 m (4 ft)
**Length:** 3.4 m (11.2 ft)
**Weight:** 85 kg (187 lb)

**DINOSAUR PROFILE**

***Tenontosaurus*, the most common plant-eater in its habitat, was often hunted by *Deinonychus*.**

*Deinonychus*'s hooked, second toe was about 13 cm (5 in) long.

*Deinonychus*'s killing method was to stab prey with its claws and then wait for it to bleed to death.

***Deinonychus* gripped its prey firmly with its claws. A kick could not shake It off.**

# Spinosaurus

The largest and longest carnivorous dinosaur, *Spinosaurus* lived in North Africa during the Cretaceous. Its pointed, crocodilian snout was perfectly shaped for snapping up fish, but this theropod also fed on dinosaurs and other land animals.

## Species and Specimens

Only a handful of fairly complete *Spinosaurus* specimens have been found—and one of those was destroyed in bombing raids on Munich, Germany, during World War II. Most dinosaur experts recognize just one species, which they call *Spinosaurus aegyptiacus* ("Egyptian spine lizard" ).

Spinosaurus had a series of tall spines sticking out of its backbone. Most experts agree this supported a sail.

## Sail or Hump?

Most paleontologists believe that the spines along *Spinosaurus's* back held up a large sail of skin. A few have another theory—that the spines supported a fatty hump, like a camel's. Either structure could have helped *Spinosaurus* to regulate its temperature, and either could have been used for display, to communicate with other dinosaurs.

| PERIOD | TRIASSIC | JURASSIC | CRETACEOUS | AGE OF MAMMALS |
|---|---|---|---|---|
| | | | 105 | |
| MILLIONS OF YEARS AGO | 251 | 206 | 145 | 65 |

present

**Name:** *Spinosaurus* (SPY-nuh-SAWR-us)
**Family:** Spinosauridae
**Height:** 6 m (20 ft)
**Length:** 16 m (52.5 ft)
**Weight:** 9 tonnes (9.9 tons)

**DINOSAUR PROFILE**

The position of its nostrils suggest that *Spinosaurus* probably spent a lot of its time underwater.

*Spinosaurus*'s narrow skull was up to 1.75 m (5.7 ft) long.

*Spinosaurus* had short, strong arms.

Primitive fish called coelacanths still exist today—but they are critically endangered.

# Tyrannosaurus

One species of *Tyrannosaurus* is more famous than any other dinosaur: *Tyrannosaurus rex*, or "king of the tyrant lizards." It inhabited North America at the end of the Cretaceous. For a long time, it was the largest known land carnivore. Today, that title goes to *Spinosaurus*.

## Search for Meat

*Tyrannosaurus* had binocular vision, which meant that it could locate prey with great accuracy. It could also move fairly quickly, thanks to its muscular back legs. Once it reached its prey, it tore into its flesh with powerful jaws. *Tyrannosaurus*'s teeth could easily crush through bone. Teeth were different sizes, but the longest were around 15 cm (6 in).

One *Tyrannosaurus* sinks its teeth into another's neck.

## Life in a Pack

Trackways in Canada show that—at least some of the time—*Tyrannosaurus* hunted in packs. As in wolf packs today, rival males probably fought each other to be pack leader. *Tyrannosaurus* would have used its fearsome jaws not only to kill prey, but to attack rivals.

| PERIOD | TRIASSIC | JURASSIC | CRETACEOUS | AGE OF MAMMALS |
|---|---|---|---|---|
| | | | 67 | |
| MILLIONS OF YEARS AGO | 251 | 206 | 145 | 65 | present |

**Name:** *Tyrannosaurus* (Tye-RAN-uh-SAWR-us)
**Family:** Tyrannosauridae
**Height:** 5.5 m (18 ft)
**Length:** 12 m (39 ft)
**Weight:** 6.1 tonnes (6.7 tons)

**DINOSAUR PROFILE**

*Tyrannosaurus* is estimated to have been able to deliver a stronger bite than any other land animal.

*Tyrannosaurus* probably had feathers for warmth.

Tail held out behind for balance

*Tyrannosaurus* walked on slim, birdlike feet. Each foot had three 18-cm- (7-in-) long claws.

*Tyrannosaurus*'s arms were short but powerful. The dinosaur scavenged and hunted.

# Melanorosaurus

One of the earliest sauropods, or long-necked plant-eating dinosaurs, *Melanorosaurus* lived between 227 and 208 mya. Its name means "Black Mountain lizard" after the place where it was first discovered: Black Mountain in Transkei, South Africa.

## First of the Line

In time, sauropods would become the largest land animals ever. Early species were much smaller—*Melanorosaurus* was just a quarter the length of *Argentinosaurus*. and far lighter. However, it was still too bulky to walk on two legs and had to lumber along on all fours.

Volcanoes were reshaping the land during the Late Triassic.

## All in the Hips

Sauropods belong to the dinosaur group called the saurischians, or lizard-hipped dinosaurs. Their hips were arranged like those of modern lizards. Sauropods were plant-eaters, but the meat-eating theropods were lizard-hipped, too. The other group of dinosaurs are the ornithischians, or bird-hipped dinosaurs. They were all plant-eaters

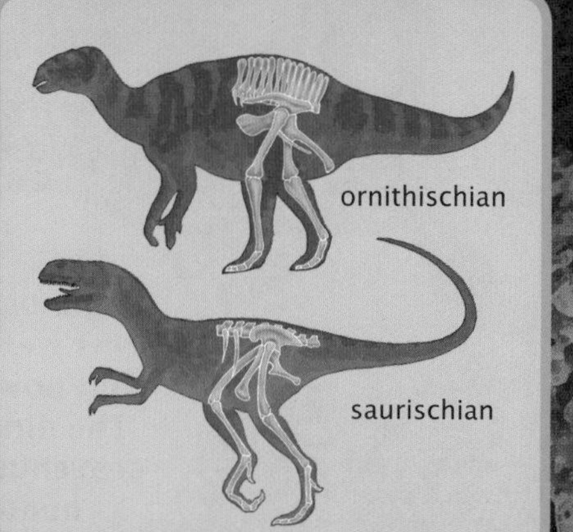


*Melanorosaurus*'s long neck allowed it to save energy. It could gather vegetation from a large area without the need to move its whole body.

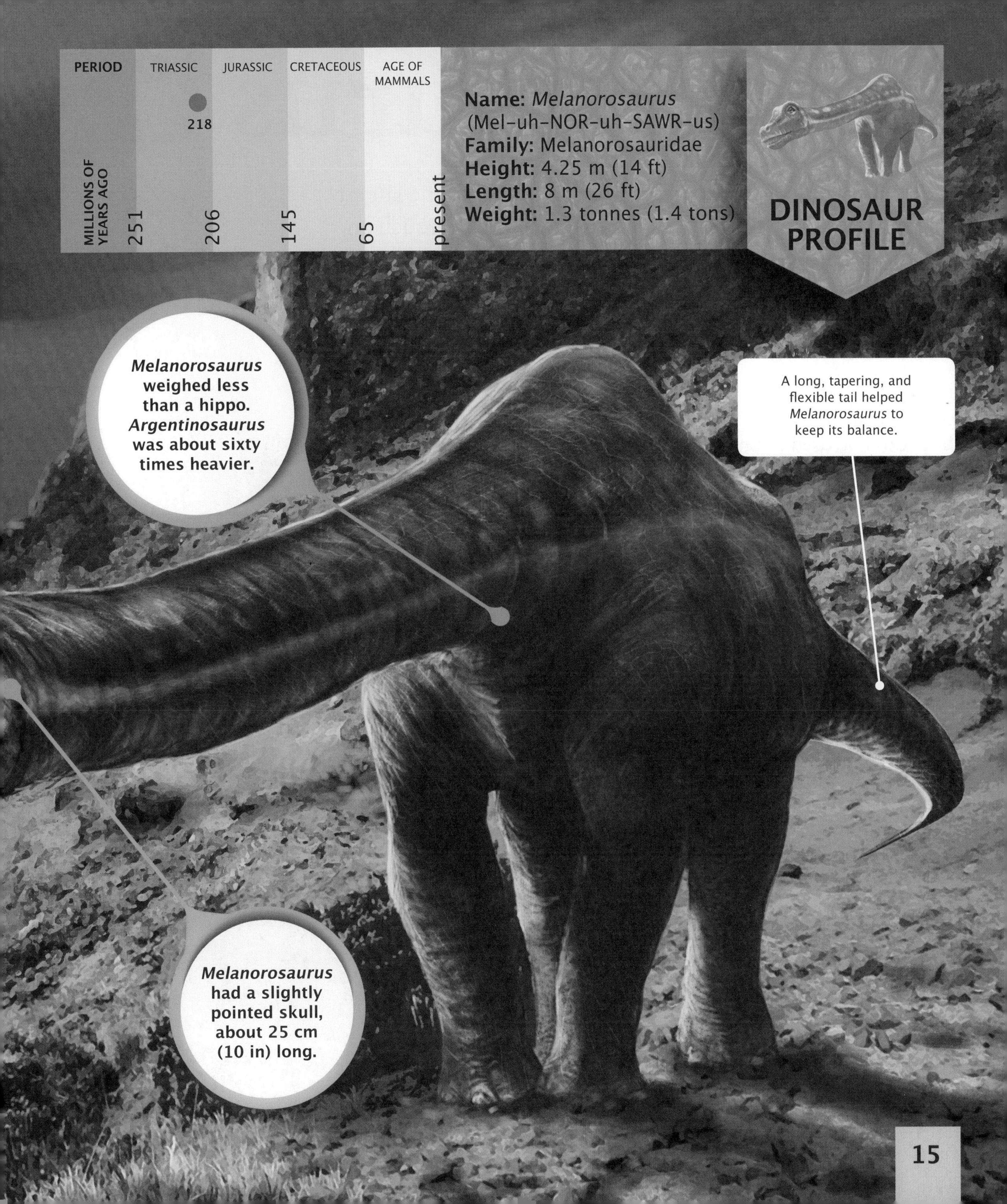


**Name:** *Melanorosaurus*
(Mel-uh-NOR-uh-SAWR-us)
**Family:** Melanorosauridae
**Height:** 4.25 m (14 ft)
**Length:** 8 m (26 ft)
**Weight:** 1.3 tonnes (1.4 tons)

# Brachiosaurus

When it was discovered in 1903, *Brachiosaurus* was the largest known dinosaur. Paleontologists did not believe that such an enormous animal could have supported its own weight on land. They thought that it must have lived in water.

## Nose Knowhow

In early reconstructions, *Brachiosaurus*'s nostrils were located on a bump between its eyes, where they could be used to breathe even when the rest of the head was submerged. Today, paleontologists know *Brachiosaurus* lived on land, not water, and position the nostrils further down the snout. The nostrils were relatively large, so the dinosaur probably had a good sense of smell.

*Brachiosaurus* had 58 leaf-shaped teeth for stripping plants of shoots, leaves, and cones.

## Eating Machines

Just like today's large herbivores, sauropods moved in herds, constantly eating and seeking out new feeding grounds. Experts estimate that *Brachiosaurus* consumed 120 kg (264 lb) of vegetation a day. Despite this, it shared its environment with other plant-eating giants, including *Apatosaurus* and *Diplodocus*.

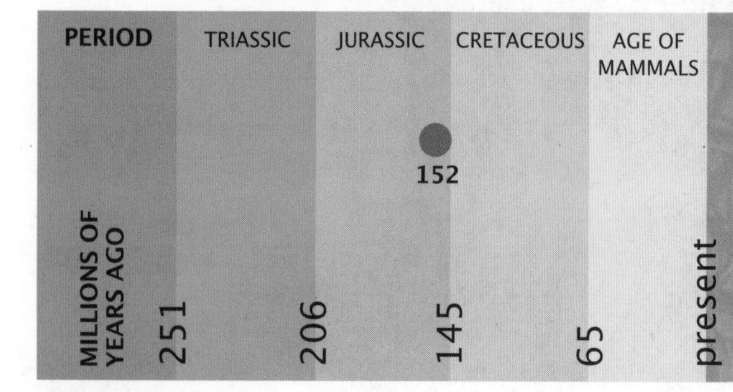


**Name:** *Brachiosaurus* (BRACK-ee-uh-SAWR-us)
**Family:** Brachiosauridae
**Height:** 9 m (30 ft)
**Length:** 30 m (98 ft)
**Weight:** 70 tonnes (77 tons)

DINOSAUR PROFILE

Unlike other sauropods, *Brachiosaurus* had longer front legs than back ones. Its back sloped down toward the tail.

***Brachiosaurus* held its neck upright, like a giraffe. One early species has since been renamed *Giraffatitan*.**

*Brachiosaurus* lived in Late Jurassic North America.

***Brachiosaurus*'s huge bulk helped it to conserve its body heat.**

# Sauroposeidon

In 1994, a few fossilized neck bones were discovered by a dog walker in Oklahoma, U.S.A. They belonged to *Sauroposeidon*. At 18 m (59 ft) high, it was the tallest known dinosaur, and almost as heavy as *Argentinosaurus*.

## Hot and Humid

Herbivorous *Sauroposeidon* lived around the shores of what is now the Gulf of Mexico 110 mya. At that time, the landscape was made up of rainforests, river deltas, and wetlands. The climate was tropical (hot and humid all year round) or subtropical (with hot, wet summers and short, mild winters).

## Swampy Habitat

*Sauroposeidon* was named after Poseidon—the Greek god of earthquakes as well as the sea—because its huge bulk would have made the ground shake. *Sauroposeidon* was the only large sauropod around at that time. The top predator was *Acrocanthosaurus*, which preyed on young *Sauroposeidon* whenever it had the opportunity.

Fossilized *Sauroposeidon* footprints have been found in Texas, U.S.A.

Like other sauropods, *Sauroposeidon* lived in herds.

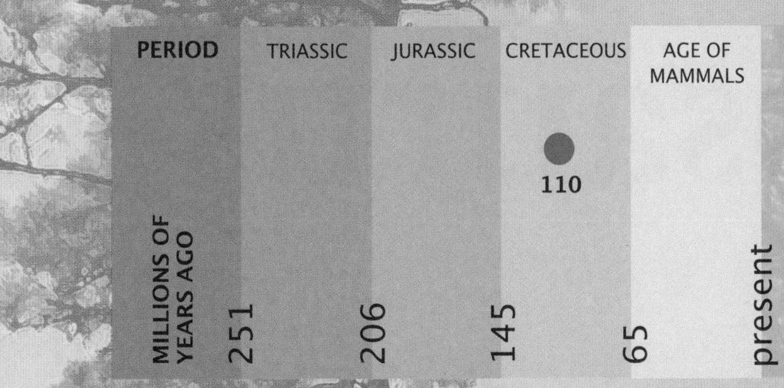


## DINOSAUR PROFILE

**Name:** *Sauroposeidon*
(SAWR-oh-puh-SIGH-don)
**Family:** Titanosauridae
**Height:** 18 m (59 ft)
**Length:** 34 m (112 ft)
**Weight:** 55 tonnes (60 tons)

**The estimated neck length was 12 m (39 ft). The largest bone, or vertebra, was a record-breaking 1.2 m (4 ft) long.**

Vegetation included palms, tree ferns, and magnolias.

***Sauroposeidon*** **juveniles may have lived with the herd for protection.**

# Argentinosaurus

The area that is now South America was warm and wet at the end of the Cretaceous, and home to some enormous, plant-eating dinosaurs. *Argentinosaurus* ("Argentina lizard") was one of the largest animals to have ever lived on land. Each of its vertebrae (spine bones) was almost as tall as a person.

Its long neck allowed the dinosaur to reach for food without moving much.

This unnamed titanosaur was even bigger than *Argentinosaurus*—as tall as a seven-storey building!

## Record-Breakers

A farmer found the first *Argentinosaurus* fossil by accident in 1987. At first, he mistook the massive leg bone for a petrified tree trunk. *Argentinosaurus* was a record-breaker for more than two decades, until a new species of titanosaur was discovered. Still unnamed, it was 40 m (131 ft) long, 20 m (66 ft) tall, and weighed 77 tonnes (85 tons).

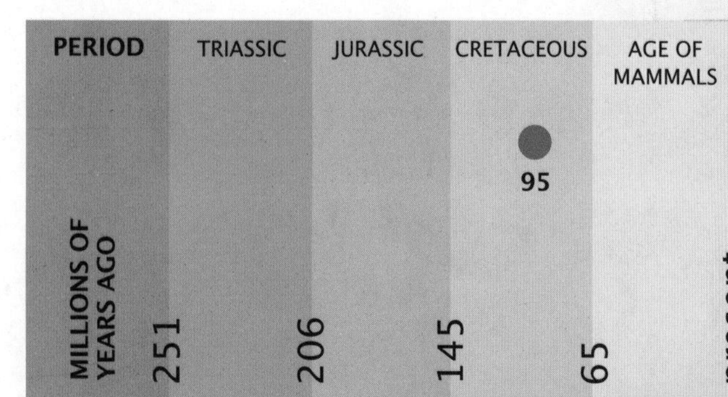


**Name:** *Argentinosaurus* (AH-gen-teen-uh-SAWR-us)
**Family:** Antarctosauridae
**Height:** 7.3 m (24 ft)
**Length:** 35 m (115 ft)
**Weight:** 73 tonnes (80 tons)

**DINOSAUR PROFILE**

## Titanosaur Teeth

*Argentinosaurus* belonged to the group of sauropods called the titanosaurs that flourished after the large Jurassic sauropods had died out. Their nostrils were set high on the snout, and they had a jaw packed with peg-like teeth.

*Argentinosaurus* probably couldn't raise its neck much above shoulder height.

The long tail stuck out behind for balance.

***Argentinosaurus* may have taken 40 years to reach its adult size.**

Thick, sturdy legs supported its heavy bulk.

# Heterodontosaurus

One of the earliest ornithischians, or bird-hipped dinosaurs. *Heterodontosaurus* lived in South Africa about 195 mya. Its name means "different toothed lizard." Unlike most reptiles, it had teeth of several different shapes.

## Tooth Types

*Heterodontosaurus*'s square cheek teeth were used for grinding and chewing. At the front of its beak-like, horny snout, it had smaller front teeth for snipping off plant stems. Finally, it had a pair of curved tusks.

*Heterodontosaurus* probably used its tusks to show off to rivals.

## Discoveries

The first *Heterodontosaurus* fossil was a skull, discovered in 1961. Five years later another skull was found—this time attached to an almost perfect skeleton. Since then, more finds have surfaced. The most complete skeleton was in 2005 but it could not be excavated because it had fossilized in such hard rock.

A cast of the *Heterodontosaurus* skeleton discovered in 1966.

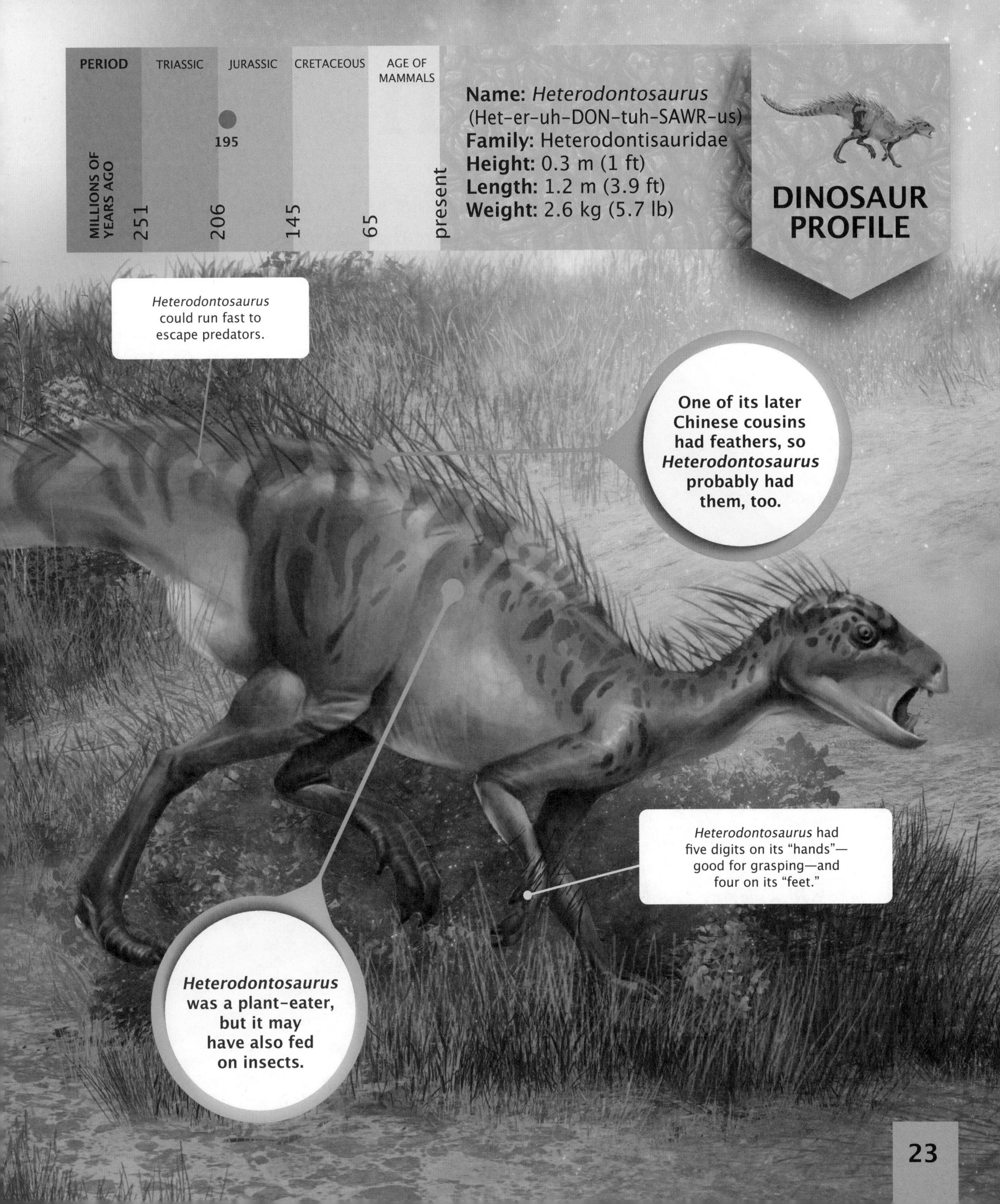
PERIOD
TRIASSIC
JURASSIC
CRETACEOUS
AGE OF MAMMALS
195
MILLIONS OF YEARS AGO
251
206
145
65
present
Name: Heterodontosaurus
(Het-er-uh-DON-tuh-SAWR-us)
Family: Heterodontisauridae
Height: 0.3 m (1 ft)
Length: 1.2 m (3.9 ft)
Weight: 2.6 kg (5.7 lb)
DINOSAUR PROFILE
Heterodontosaurus could run fast to escape predators.
One of its later Chinese cousins had feathers, so Heterodontosaurus probably had them, too.
Heterodontosaurus had five digits on its "hands"—good for grasping—and four on its "feet."
Heterodontosaurus was a plant-eater, but it may have also fed on insects.

# Iguanodon

*Iguanodon* walked on all fours, with its body and tail parallel to the ground.

The large plant-eater *Iguanodon* roamed across Europe and North America during the Early and Mid Cretaceous. More than 25 species are known. *Iguanodon* moved in herds for protection against predators such as *Deinonychus*.

**Some experts think that *Iguanodon* may have had cheek pouches for storing food.**

***Iguanodon* sometimes reared up to reach for food or look for danger.**

## Eating Technique

*Iguanodon* had a toothless beak for cropping off tough horsetails and ferns, and wide cheek teeth for mashing and pulping plant matter. The teeth were similar to a modern-day iguana's (*Iguanodon* means "iguana tooth").

*Iguanodon*'s tail stuck out stiffly behind it.

*Iguanodon* had a vicious thumb spike to stab at would-be attackers.

## Early Finds

*Iguanodon* was only the second dinosaur to be named (the first was *Megalosaurus*). The first fossils were a few teeth from southern England. The most spectacular finds came from a coal mine at Bernissart in Belgium. Nearly 40 *Iguanodon* skeletons were uncovered there in 1878.

An *Iguanodon* skeleton from Bernissart, Belgium, being mounted for display

| PERIOD | TRIASSIC | JURASSIC | CRETACEOUS | AGE OF MAMMALS |
|---|---|---|---|---|
| | | | ● 121 | |
| MILLIONS OF YEARS AGO | 251 | 206 | 145 | 65 | present |

**Name:** *Iguanodon* (Ig-WAN-oh-don)
**Family:** Iguanodontidae
**Height:** 3.25 m (10.7 ft)
**Length:** 10 m (33 ft)
**Weight:** 3.1 tonnes (3.4 tons)

**DINOSAUR PROFILE**

# Parasaurolophus

One of the hadrosaurs, or duck-billed dinosaurs, herbivorous *Parasaurolophus* lived across North America around 75 mya. It was thought to be a close relative of another hadrosaur, *Saurolophus* ("crested lizard"). *Parasaurolophus* means "like *Saurolophus*."

The crest made its calls travel further.

## Skull Features

In fact, *Saurolophus*'s crest was mostly solid, while *Parasaurolophus*'s was hollow. It had tubes leading to and from the nostrils and amplified the dinosaur's calls (made them louder). *Parasaurolophus*'s closest relative was the large Asian hadrosaur *Charonosaurus*.

*Parasaurolophus* went up on two legs to run or look out for danger.

***Parasaurolophus*'s short, stout legs helped it to push through thick undergrowth.**

*Parasaurolophus* grazed on all fours.

## Hot Head

Some paleontologists believe that *Parasaurolophus*'s crest helped it to keep its body temperature steady. It could have soaked up heat during the daytime to keep *Parasaurolophus* warm at night. Another possibility is that *Parasaurolophus* could lose excess body heat through its crest, to stop it becoming too hot.

Including the crest, *Parasaurolophus*'s skull could be more than 2 m (6.6 ft) long, depending on the species.

*Parasaurolophus* communicated with members of the herd to warn of predators or to attract a mate.

**The crest grew larger with age. It may have looked different in males and females.**

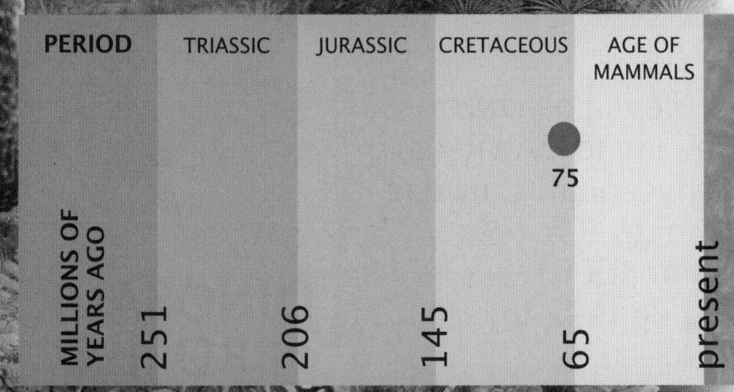


**Name:** *Parasaurolophus* (Par-ah-SAWR-OL-uh-fus)
**Family:** Hadrosauridae
**Height:** 3.6 m (12 ft)
**Length:** 11 m (36 ft)
**Weight:** 2.5 tonnes (2.8 tons)

**DINOSAUR PROFILE**

# Pachycephalosaurus

The pachycephalosaurs are named after *Pachycephalosaurus*, a dome-headed dinosaur from Late Cretaceous North America. Paleontologists once thought that these plant-eaters bashed their heads together like goats. However, it is unlikely that they fought each other head-to-head.

*Pachycephalosaurus* walked and ran on two legs, but would have foraged on all fours.

## Protective Helmet

The solid bone at the top of the skull protected *Pachycephalosaurus*'s delicate brain when it charged headfirst at full speed. The bone was 25 cm (10 in) thick in places.

*Pachycephalosaurus*'s jaw had tiny, sharp teeth for eating soft fruit, seeds, and young leaves.

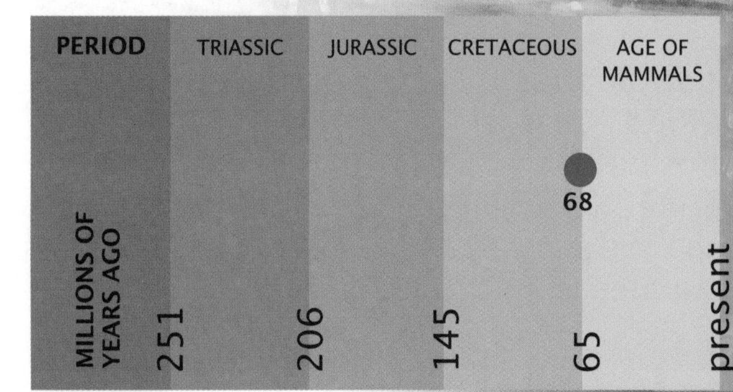


Name: *Pachycephalosaurus* (Pak-ee-SEF-uh-lo-SAWR-us)
**Family:** Pachycephalosauridae
**Height:** 1.8 m (5.9 ft)
**Length:** 4.5 m (15 ft)
**Weight:** 450 kg (992 lb)

**DINOSAUR PROFILE**

Large eyes gave *Pachycephalosaurus* good binocular vision.

***Pachycephalosaurus* used its head to charge into rivals' thighs.**

**There was a circle of bony spikes around the bottom of the skull dome; there were also spikes at the end of the snout.**

*Pachycephalosaurus* had long legs and short arms. It was not a fast runner.

## Fossil Discoveries

*Pachycephalosaurus* was named in 1931. Not many fossils have been found—just one skull, some skull roofs, and a few other bones. In 2016 paleontologists announced that they had found skulls from two baby *Pachycephalosaurus* at the Hell Creek Formation in Montana, U.S.A.

# Protoceratops

A spectacular fossil discovered in 1971 in the Gobi Desert, Mongolia, captured two dinosaurs locked in combat. They had been buried alive. One was the plant-eating, primitive ceratopsian *Protoceratops*; the other was the dromaeosaur *Velociraptor*.

*Protoceratops* and *Velociraptor* had been preserved in sand mid-fight. Experts believe they were caught up in a sudden sandstorm.

## Life in the Gobi

Many *Protoceratops* specimens have been found in the red sandstone of the Gobi Desert, including fossilized nests, eggs, and babies. During the Late Cretaceous, the Gobi was not as dry as it is now. There were probably seasonal floods.

*Protoceratops* used its wide, spade-like claws to dig nests and burrows. It laid up to 15 eggs at a time.

**Like all dromaeosaurs, *Velociraptor* had a killer curved claw on the second toe of each foot. It slashed at prey to make it bleed to death.**

| PERIOD | TRIASSIC | JURASSIC | CRETACEOUS | AGE OF MAMMALS |
|---|---|---|---|---|
| | | | 73 | |
| MILLIONS OF YEARS AGO | 251 | 206 | 145 | 65 | present |

**Name:** *Protoceratops* (Pro-toe-SEH-ruh-tops)
**Family:** Ceratopsidae
**Height:** 70 cm (27.6 in)
**Length:** 1.9 m (6.2 ft)
**Weight:** 180 kg (397 lb)

**DINOSAUR PROFILE**

This fossil of a newly hatched *Protoceratops andrewsi* was discovered in 1997.

## Desert Discoveries

The first *Protoceratops* specimens were discovered in the 1920s by American paleontologist Roy Chapman Andrews, so they were given the species name *andrewsi*. In 2001, a second species was identified, *Protoceratops hellenikorhinus*. Unlike *Protoceratops andrewsi*, it had two nose horns, but no front teeth.

*Protoceratops* had a relatively large neck frill, probably for display.

*Velociraptor* was about the same size as *Protoceratops*.

***Protoceratops*'s tough, horny beak was not powerful enough to damage *Velociraptor*.**

# Triceratops

The neck frill might have helped *Triceratops* keep its temperature steady. It was also for display.

One of the biggest ceratopsians, *Triceratops* lived right at the end of the Cretaceous in what is now North America. Its most striking feature was its three horns—a longer pair above its eyes and a shorter one on its nose.

## Skull Features

*Triceratops*'s skull was massive. Its horns and neck frill were both used for display—showing off to possible mates, fighting rivals, and perhaps even allowing herd members to identify each other. The dinosaur also used its horns to defend against predatory tyrannosaurs.

*Triceratops*'s skull was around 2 m (6.6 ft) long—about a quarter of its total body length.

| PERIOD | TRIASSIC | JURASSIC | CRETACEOUS | AGE OF MAMMALS |
|---|---|---|---|---|
| | | | 67 | |
| MILLIONS OF YEARS AGO 251 | 206 | 145 | 65 | present |

**Name:** *Triceratops* (Try-SEH-ruh-tops)
**Family:** Ceratopsidae
**Height:** 3 m (10 ft)
**Length:** 8.5 m (28 ft)
**Weight:** 8 tonnes (8.8 tons)

DINOSAUR PROFILE

*Triceratops* had up to 800 cheek teeth. Cycads and palms quickly wore them down, but they were constantly being replaced.

## Prehistoric Elephants?

For more than a century, all the *Triceratops* fossils were of solitary animals. Then, in 2009, paleontologists found three juveniles together. It is possible that *Triceratops* lived in social groups, just as African elephants do. Like them, *Triceratops* was a plant-eater and could have used its bulky body to knock down big bushes.

Each brow horn was around 1 m (3 ft) long.

***Triceratops* used its brow horns to fight rival males.**

The beak-like mouth could snap tough plant stems.

# Scutellosaurus

Appearing in the Early Jurassic, *Scutellosaurus* was an ancestor of the later shielded dinosaurs, such as *Ankylosaurus* and *Stegosaurus*. The name *Scutellosaurus* means "lizard with little shields."

The speedy theropod *Coelophysis* would have hunted *Scutellosaurus*.

## Little Darter

*Scutellosaurus* was a plant-eater that lived in what is now Arizona, in the southern United States. Small and lightly built, it had longer back legs than front ones, so it probably moved around on two legs. Its small skull housed a small brain.

## The Shield Bearers

*Scutellosaurus* belonged to a group of dinosaurs called the thyreophorans, or "shield bearers." Their skin had evolved to protect them from attack. Early thyreophorans, such as *Scutellosaurus*, simply had bony bumps, called osteoderms. By the Late Cretaceous, the group included ankylosaurs and stegosaurs, which had elaborate plates and spikes.

*Scutellosaurus* probably went down on all fours to eat shrubby plants.

*Scutellosaurus*'s back was studded with bony scales called osteoderms.

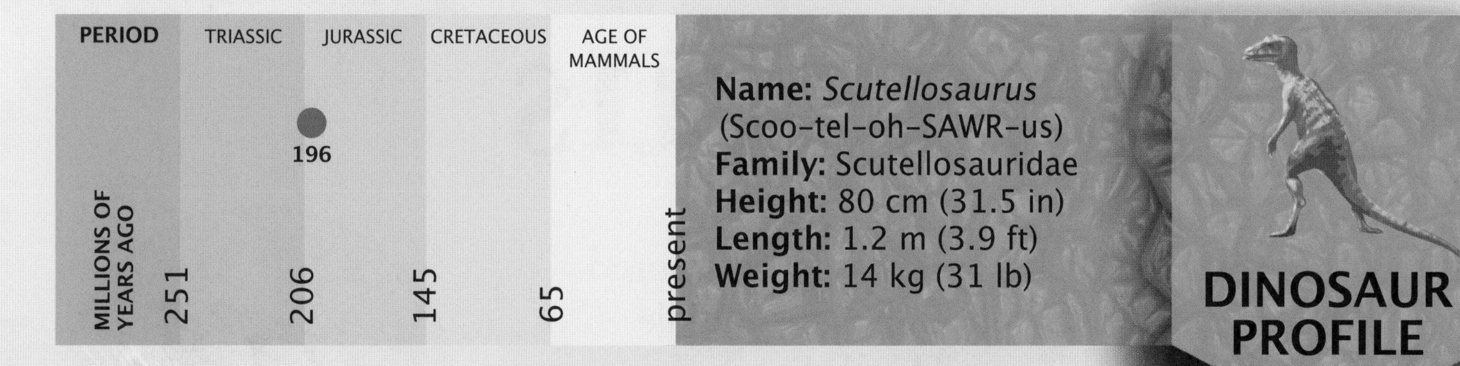


*Scutellosaurus* probably had fleshy cheeks, like most other ornithischians.

**Scutellosaurus's long, thin tail helped it to balance. It made up more than half of its body length.**

Dragonflies and other insects probably made up part of *Scutellosaurus*'s diet.

**The rows of osteoderms made it hard for predators to sink their teeth or claws into the skin.**

# Stegosaurus

Stegosaurs are all named after *Stegosaurus*, which ranged across North America and Europe during the Middle Jurassic. This herbivore had a small head, diamond-shaped plates along its back, and a defensive, spiky tail.

## Lethal Weapon

The group of spikes at the end of a stegosaur's tail is called a thagomizer. It was *Stegosaurus*'s only protection against predators. The dinosaur swung and flicked its tail, hoping to hit an attacker and inflict serious damage.

*Stegosaurus*'s skull was long and narrow.

**Unlike other known stegosaurs, *Stegosaurus*'s plates were staggered instead of in pairs.**

## All about Plates

Early reconstructions of *Stegosaurus* had its plates flat on top of its body—that is how the dinosaur got its name, which means "roofed lizard." Paleontologists now know that the plates stood upright, making the dinosaur look bigger than it was. They were almost certainly for display, but they may have also helped *Stegosaurus* to regulate its body temperature.

*Stegosaurus* probably used its plates to show off to other members of the same species.

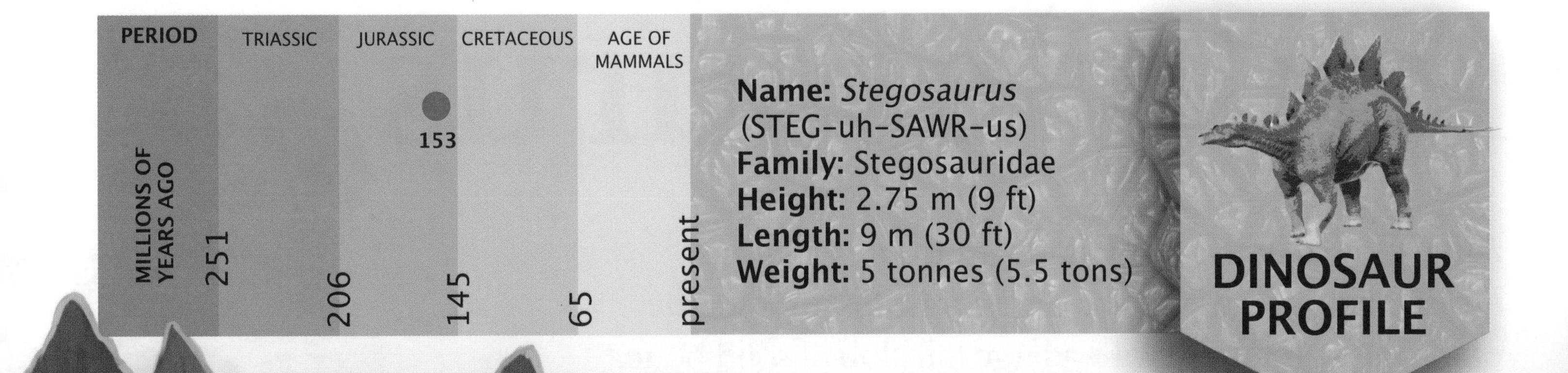


**Name:** *Stegosaurus* (STEG-uh-SAWR-us)
**Family:** Stegosauridae
**Height:** 2.75 m (9 ft)
**Length:** 9 m (30 ft)
**Weight:** 5 tonnes (5.5 tons)

## DINOSAUR PROFILE

***Stegosaurus*'s small skull housed a hotdog-shaped brain.**

*Ornitholestes* hunted in packs.

*Stegosaurus* could not move fast because of its short front legs. Its top speed was 7 km/h (4.3 mph).

*Ornitholestes* was a 12.6-kg (27.8-lb) theropod that lived in North America at the same time as *Stegosaurus*.

# Ankylosaurus

Ankylosaurs all take their name from *Ankylosaurus* ("fused lizard"). It was the largest ankylosaur and one of the best-protected, with a large tail club of solid bone.

## Terrifying Threats

*Ankylosaurus* lived in North America at the end of the Cretaceous. This herbivore shared its habitat with one of the most terrifying hunters of all time—*Tyrannosaurus*. However, an adult *Ankylosaurus* could have swung its tail club with enough force to break *Tyrannosaurus*'s leg.

## Big Head

*Ankylosaurus*'s skull had many air passages running through it that made it bulge out at the sides. Paleontologists are still not sure what these passages were for. They may have helped with the dinosaur's sense of smell or they may have amplified its calls (made them louder).

Four head spikes protected *Ankylosaurus*'s face.

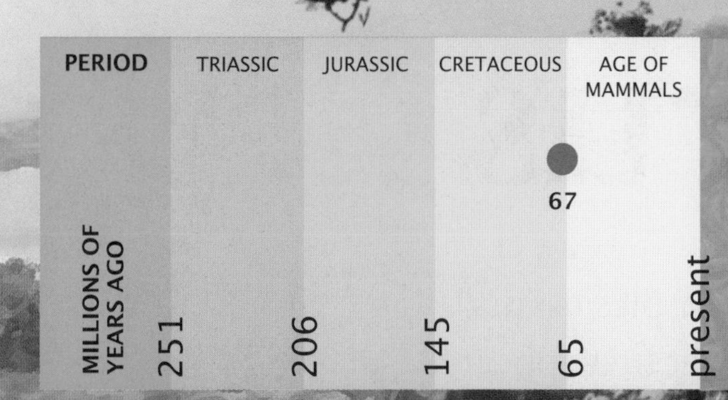


Name: *Ankylosaurus* (Ang-KILE-uh-SAWR-us)
**Family:** Ankylosauridae
**Height:** 1.7 m (5.6 ft)
**Length:** 6.25 m (20.5 ft)
**Weight:** 6 tonnes (6.6 tons)

## DINOSAUR PROFILE

**Hundreds of bite-proof bony plates covered *Ankylosaurus*'s upper body.**

**The tail club was made of fused bone.**

*Ankylosaurus*'s jaw housed tiny teeth.

# Plesiosaurus

Many types of reptile lived in Mesozoic oceans. The plesiosaurs were a group of long-necked swimming reptiles that first appeared in the Late Triassic and died out at the end of the Cretaceous. They are named after *Plesiosaurus* (the "close lizard").

## Life in the Water

*Plesiosaurus* lived in shallow waters, close to the coast. It's possible it came ashore to lay its eggs, like today's turtles. It could not have moved quickly on land, because it had flippers instead of legs. Plesiosaurs evolved from nothosaurs, Triassic, four-legged reptiles whose feet had adapted to swimming in the water by being webbed and paddle-like.

*Kaiwhekea* was one of the last plesiosaurs. A specialist squid hunter, it grew to 7 m (23 ft) long.

*Meyerasaurus* lived in the Early Jurassic. It was about the same length as *Plesiosaurus*.

## Short-Necked Cousins

Not all plesiosaurs had long necks. Pliosaurs, including *Kronosaurus* were plesiosaurs with shorter necks and bigger heads. Pliosaurs also had slightly larger back flippers than front ones (in most plesiosaurs, the front flippers were larger). All plesiosaurs shared the same feeding technique, however—snapping up fish and squid as they moved their head from side to side.

*Plesiosaurus* had a small head. It had small, sharp teeth for gripping slippery prey, such as squid.

The 2-m- (6.6-ft-) long shark *Hybodus* shared the seas with *Plesiosaurus.*

Plesiosaurs hunted extinct mollusks called ammonites.

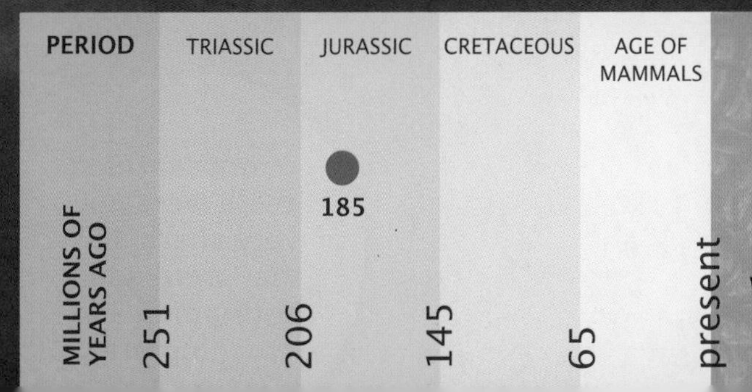


**Name:** *Plesiosaurus* (Plee-zee-oh-SAWR-us)
**Family:** Plesiosauridae
**Length:** 3.5 m (11.4 ft)
**Weight:** 450 kg (992 lb)

## MARINE REPTILE PROFILE

# Kronosaurus

One of the largest pliosaurs, 10-m- (33-ft-) long *Kronosaurus* lived in the Early Cretaceous. It powered through the water after turtles and other plesiosaurs, snapping them up in its huge jaws.

## Built for Speed

Pliosaurs had muscular bodies, short necks, and long heads. The short tail kept them streamlined and they swam by moving all four flippers at once. They were fast-moving and usually outswam prey. Once they had caught their victim, they shook it in their jaws and swallowed it whole.

Pliosaurs are named after the Late Jurassic marine reptile, *Pliosaurus*.

***Kronosaurus*'s teeth were not very sharp, but they were good at gripping and crushing prey.**

The pointed tail helped the body slip through the water without creating any drag.

## History of Discovery

The first *Kronosaurus* fossils—teeth dug up in Australia in 1899—were not identified as *Kronosaurus* until the 1920s. For decades the pliosaur was known only in Australia. In 1994, paleontologists announced that a fossil had been found in Colombia, South America. *Kronosaurus* probably lived in shallow seas worldwide.

**Pliosaurs "flew" through the water using their four wing-like flippers.**

*Kronosaurus*'s longest teeth were around 30 cm (11.8 in) long. Even the shortest were more than 7 cm (2.8 in).

| PERIOD | TRIASSIC | JURASSIC | CRETACEOUS | AGE OF MAMMALS | |
|---|---|---|---|---|---|
| MILLIONS OF YEARS AGO | 251 | 206 | 145 | 65 | present |
| | | | 112 | | |

**Name:** *Kronosaurus* (KROH-nuh-SAWR-us)
**Family:** Pliosauridae
**Length:** 10 m (33 ft)
**Weight:** 8.2 tonnes (9 tons)

**MARINE REPTILE PROFILE**

# Dimorphodon

The pterosaurs, or "winged lizards," were flying reptiles that appeared in the Late Triassic, around 200 mya. *Dimorphodon* was an average-sized pterosaur that lived during the Early Jurassic. Its head looked like a puffin's.

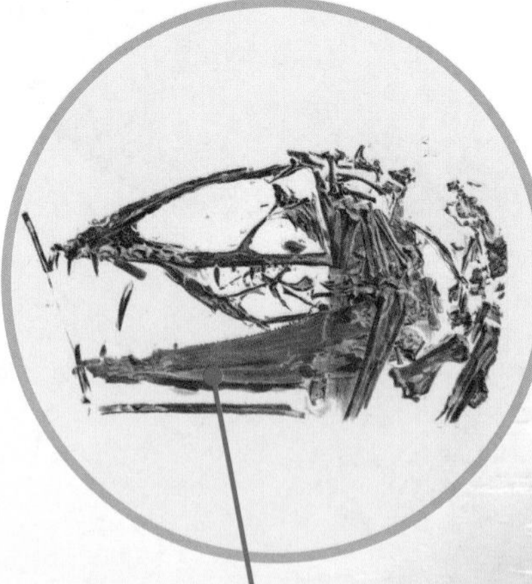

This drawing of *Dimorphodon*'s skull appeared in Richard Owen's *A History of British Fossil Reptiles* (1849–84).

## Coastal Lifestyle

*Dimorphodon* could fly, but not for long distances. It probably lived along coasts, climbing cliffs or moving about on all fours. It caught its main food—insects—by snapping its jaws shut very fast. It also ate fish, small animals, and carrion.

## Wings and Flight

Pterosaurs were the first vertebrates (animals with backbones) that were capable of powered flight. Their wings, which were made of skin, muscle, and other tissues, stretched from their long fourth finger down to their ankles.

*Dimorphodon*'s wingspan was about the same as a buzzard's.

**The deep jaws contained up to 40 small, sharp teeth and two larger, stabbing, front teeth.**

**Name:** *Dimorphodon* (Dye-MAW-fuh-don)
**Family:** Dimorphodontidae
**Length:** 1 m (3.3 ft)
**Wingspan:** 1.4 m (4.6 ft)
**Weight:** 2.3 kg (5 lb)

## PTEROSAUR PROFILE

**A diamond-shaped flap at the end of *Dimorphodon*'s tail helped it to steer when flying.**

*Dimorphodon* may have cared for its young like this, or it may have left them to fend for themselves.

*Dimorphodon* had two types of teeth (its name means "two teeth shapes").

# Quetzalcoatlus

Named after Quetzalcoatl, the feathered serpent god of Aztec mythology, *Quetzalcoatlus* lived at the end of the Cretaceous. Its wingspan was up to 11 m (36 ft), making it the largest of the 150 known species of pterosaur.

## On the Lookout

*Quetzalcoatlus* had a long neck and good eyesight. On land it walked on all fours, looking for carrion or small animals to eat. Flight used a lot of energy. Wherever possible, *Quetzalcoatlus* glided rather than flapping its wings.

The wing membrane was thin but tough; it was just 23 cm (8 in) thick at the elbows.

## Taking Off

Smaller pterosaurs could launch themselves into the air by running along on their back legs, like birds. Larger ones, such as *Quetzalcoatlus*, were too heavy for that and needed to start from a quadrupedal position. Their front legs were much stronger than their back ones, and could give enough of an upward thrust to make the animal airborne.

Pterosaurs did not have feathers. However some, perhaps including *Quetzalcoatlus*, had fuzzy filaments called pycnofibers covering their bodies.

| PERIOD | TRIASSIC | JURASSIC | CRETACEOUS | AGE OF MAMMALS |
|---|---|---|---|---|
| | | | ● 67 | |
| MILLIONS OF YEARS AGO | 251 | 206 | 145 | 65 | present |

**Name:** *Quetzalcoatlus* (Kwet-zel-KWAT-al-us)
**Family:** Azhdarchidae
**Height:** 4.9 m (16 ft)
**Wingspan:** 11 m (36 ft)
**Weight:** 225 kg (496 lb)

## PTEROSAUR PROFILE

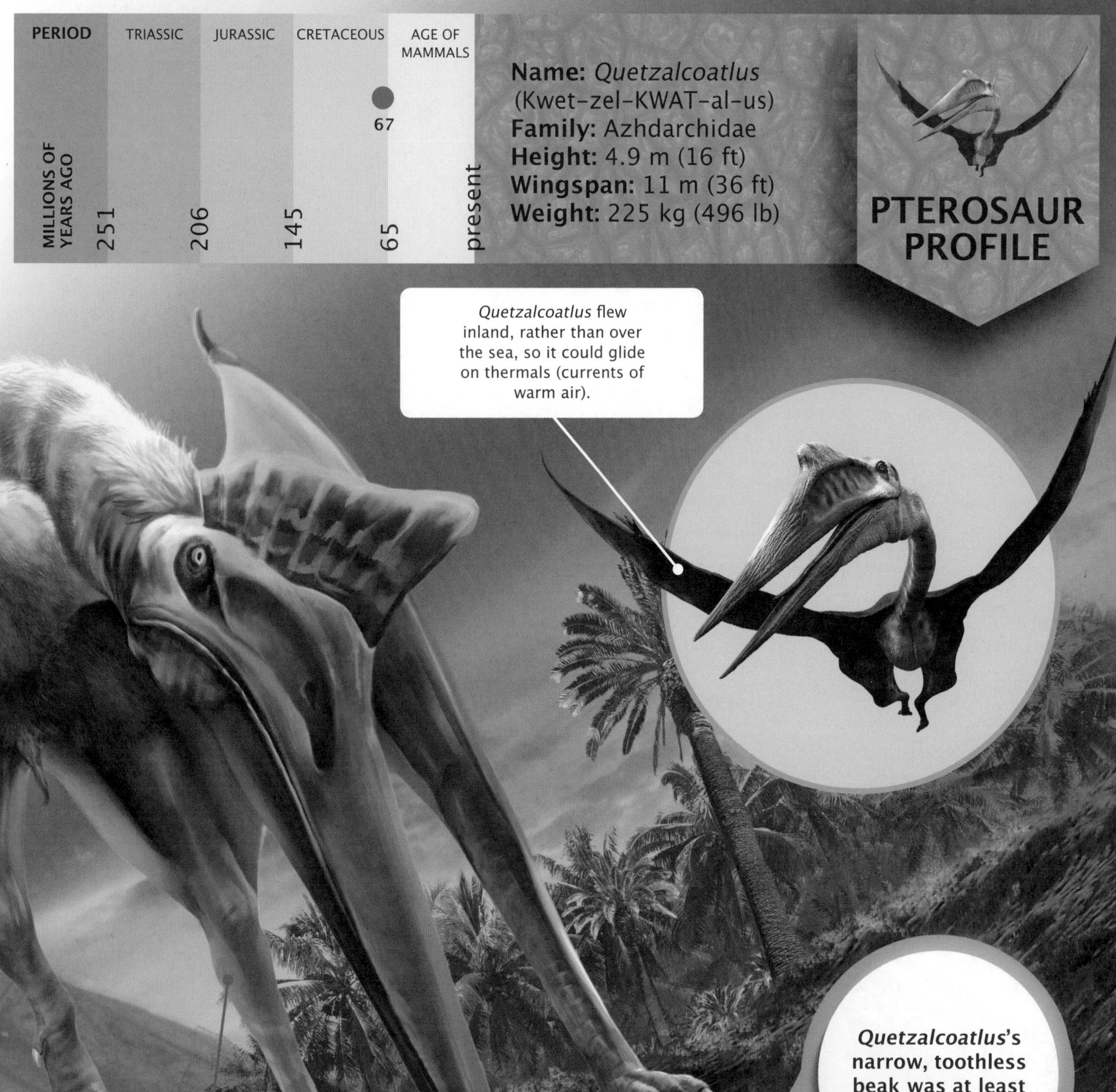

*Quetzalcoatlus* flew inland, rather than over the sea, so it could glide on thermals (currents of warm air).

***Quetzalcoatlus*'s narrow, toothless beak was at least 2.5 m (8 ft) long.**

The back legs were probably the first to touch the ground when *Quetzalcoatlus* landed.

# Glossary

ALLOSAUR
A large theropod with a long, narrow skull, usually with ornamental horns or crests.

BIPEDAL
Walking on two legs.

CARNIVORE
A meat-eater.

CARRION
Rotting flesh from a dead animal.

CERATOPSIAN
A dinosaur with (usually) horns and frills. Early species were bipedal; later ones were large and quadrupedal.

CRETACEOUS PERIOD
The time from 145 to 65 mya.

DIPLODOCID
A very long sauropod with relatively short legs.

DROMAEOSAUR
A small theropod with an outsized claw on each back foot.

EXTINCT
Describes an animal or plant that has disappeared forever.

FOSSIL
The remains of an animal or plant that died long ago, preserved in rock.

HERBIVORE
A plant-eater.

ICHTHYOSAUR
A dolphin-like, predatory marine reptile of the Mesozoic.

JURASSIC PERIOD
The time from 206 to 145 mya.

MESOZOIC ERA
The period of geological time from 251 to 65 mya.

ORNITHOPOD
An ornithischian dinosaur with a bony, beak-like mouth.

PALEONTOLOGIST
A scientist who studies fossils.

PREDATOR
An animal that hunts and eats other animals for food.

PREY
An animal that is hunted and eaten by other animals for food.

PROSAUROPOD
A primitive sauropod.

QUADRUPEDAL
Walking on all four legs.

SCAVENGE
To eat carrion or leftover kills from other hunters.

SERRATED
Having a notched, knife-like edge.

SPECIES
One particular type of living thing. Members of the same species look similar and can produce offspring together.

THEROPOD
A bipedal saurischian dinosaur with sharp teeth and claws.

TITANOSAUR
A huge sauropod with a relatively small head.

TRIASSIC PERIOD
The time from 251 to 206 mya.

TYRANNOSAUR
A large theropod with a huge head and relatively small arms.

WINGSPAN
The width of a flying animal's outstretched wings, from wing tip to wing tip.